LOWCOUNTRY
A to Z

Written by Betsy Strickland

Photography by Eric Horan

For my family and the far too few unhurried moments we share...
and for my husband, Arnold: for your patience, love and support. - B.S.

For my wife, Jan, without her love and support, I surely would not still be in business.
Also to our future grandkids and all our nieces and nephews
who will have the chance to enjoy and learn from this book. - E.H.

This book is intended to provide a glimpse into just some of the wonders of the lowcountry.
Please refer the following books for further information and insight.

Ballantine, Todd. *Tideland Treasure*. Hilton Head Island, SC. Deerfield Publishing, 1983.

Burn, Billie. *An Island Named Daufuskie*. Spartanburg, SC: The Reprint Company in association with Billie Burn Books, 1991.

Horan, Eric. *Carolina Nature: A photographer's view of the natural history in the Carolinas*. Beaufort, SC. Southern Light Photographic, 2003.

Meyer, Peter. *Nature Guide to the North Carolina Coast*. Wilmington, NC: Avian-Cetacean Press, 1998.

Parker, Leslie E. Jr. *The Hilton Head Dolphin Book*. Hilton Head Island, SC. Streeter Printing & Graphics, 1995.

Makai Concepts, LLC
PO Box 21644
Hilton Head Island, SC 29925
www.lowcountryatoz.com

Printed and bound in China
Four Colour Imports Ltd.

10 9 8 7 6 5 4 3 2 1

Publisher's Cataloging-in-Publication Data

Strickland, Betsy, 1966 –
Lowcountry A to Z / by Betsy Strickland;
photography Eric Horan.
Summary: Presents information about the South Carolina Lowcountry in an alphabetical arrangement.
ISBN 0-9744035-0-4
        1.South Carolina – Juvenile literature. 2. English language – Alphabet – Juvenile Literature.
            {1. South Carolina. 2. Alphabet.}

975.7 — dc21   2003112000

Introduction

I wrote this book for several reasons. The most important reason was to give my children, and all children of the lowcountry (young and old), an answer to some of the simplest questions about our unique environment and our surroundings.

Another reason why I wrote this book was to share the wonder of the lowcountry with children all over the world. We are so blessed to live in this area. I wanted others to experience the magnificence that we are so fortunate to enjoy every day.

Finally, I wrote this book to make sure that we do, in fact, enjoy the lowcountry each and every day... so that we don't become complacent and take her charms for granted, so that we may always live under her magical spell.

I hope that you learn something new as you read this book. My wish is that you will share this book and this new knowledge with your own family. My plea is for us all to take care of our environment and surroundings by treating them with respect as part of our own extended families.

Betsy Strickland

Acknowledgements

Kim Washok-Jones
Vice-President of Science
Coastal Discovery Museum
Hilton Head Island, SC
www.coastaldiscovery.org

Robert A. Mogil, M.D.
Member - Audubon Society
Hilton Head Island Chapter

Aa is for alligator

Alligators are frequently seen on Hilton Head Island. Alligators can be seen sunbathing on the banks of lagoons or swimming in the water. The American Alligator can grow up to 12 feet long and weigh over 400 pounds. Though alligators are large in size, they are surprisingly quick and can outrun even a horse for a limited distance. Alligators have a slow digestion. They usually eat only one pound of food a week such as fish and other small animals. In the winter months, alligators hibernate in underground dens they dig in the side of the banks of lagoons. Alligators should not be disturbed and they should not be fed; in fact, it is against the law by the Department of Natural Resources!

Bb is for bridge

Bridges are the link between the mainland and the barrier islands of the lowcountry. In 1956, the first bridge to Hilton Head Island was built. The James F. Byrnes Bridge, a two-lane toll swing bridge, was built which replaced the original means of mass transportation to the island: ferryboats! Bridges are a sight to marvel at, providing functional yet awe-inspiring access across the waterways. Two such bridges in the lowcountry are the Talmadge Memorial Bridge in Savannah, GA and the Cooper River Bridge in Charleston, SC; both of which are modern cable-stayed bridges. In fact, the Cooper River Bridge is the largest cable-stayed bridge in the United States!

Cc is for crab

Crabs abound in the lowcountry: blue crabs, fiddler crabs, ghost crabs, and hermit crabs are just some of the local species. Crabs are crustaceans meaning they have a hard shell. To go "crabbing" is to try to catch a crab in a net or cage using bait such as fish, chicken, or even corn. If you are lucky, you just might catch your dinner! Blue crabs are the most common edible crab on the Atlantic shore; the sweet white meat must be carefully picked from the shell. A surprising creature is the Horseshoe Crab because it is not a crab at all but a relative of the spider family. His spiked tail is not a weapon; it provides balance for swimming. In addition, the blood of the horseshoe crab is used extensively in medical research because it contains copper instead of iron.

Dd is for dolphin

Dolphins are often seen swimming in the ocean or bays in groups of four to six called pods. These Atlantic Bottle-Nosed dolphins are actually warm-blooded mammals, not fish. They usually hold their breath for only three minutes so you can see them as they surface or come to the top of the water to breathe, which they must do even while they are sleeping. They locate their food, mostly fish, and communicate with each other, by echolocation, which is like sonar. Dolphins are very friendly creatures and will approach boats, especially if encouraged by banging on the side of your boat. In 1993, a federal law was passed as an amendment to the Marine Mammal Protection Act of 1972, which prohibits feeding dolphins because feeding dolphins interferes with their natural eating cycle making them more dependent on humans.

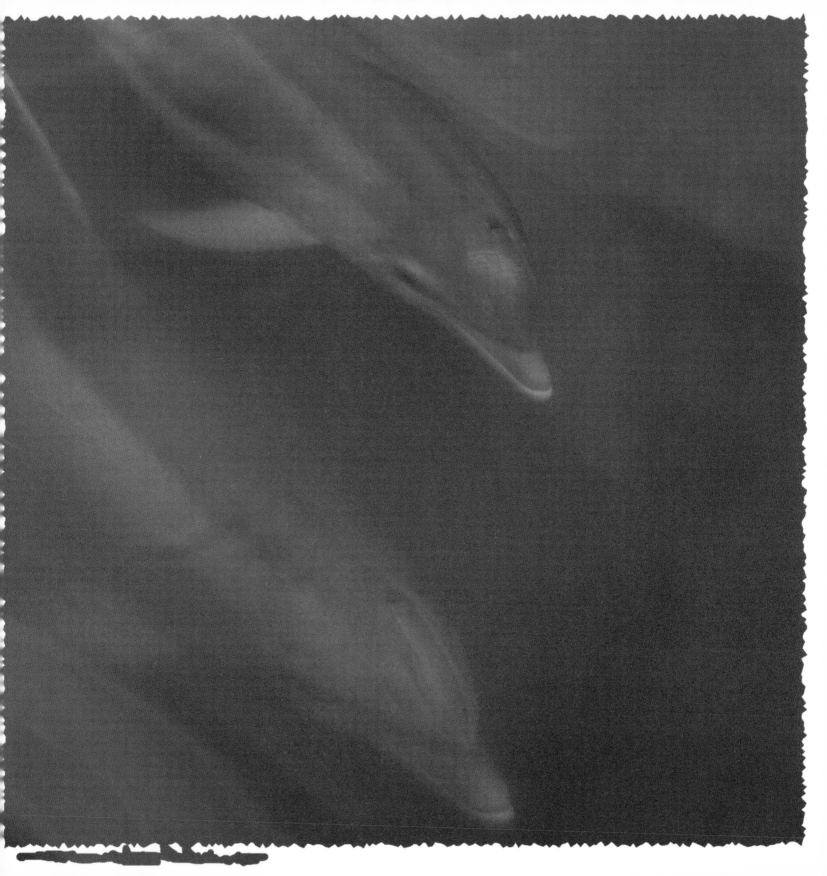

Ee is for egret

Egrets are the magnificent white birds often seen near the water's edge. The Great White Egret has a yellow beak and is slightly larger than the Snowy Egret. The Great Blue Heron is another striking bird that can stand up to 4 feet tall. Both the egret and the heron like to eat seafood just like humans do; their favorites are fish, crabs, shrimp, and even an occasional frog! A most unusual bird is the double-crested Cormorant and his cousin the Anhinga, also known as the "snake-bird." They can be seen swimming in lagoons then diving underwater for their food. After swimming, they sit on the banks to dry their wings because their feathers lack the waterproof oil that other birds such as ducks and geese possess. The Osprey, often confused with an eagle, is another magnificent bird that can be seen nesting near bridges or utility towers bringing fish to its young.

Ff is for fishing

Fishing is a favorite pastime in the lowcountry. Try your luck fishing from local docks, the beach, or on a chartered deep-sea fishing trip. Common ocean fish include mullet, cobia, red snapper, flounder, and grouper. Another popular ocean fish is the dolphinfish, also known by its Hawaiian nickname Mahi-Mahi. The dolphinfish is not actually a dolphin or porpoise though its name has fooled more than a few people! In the freshwater rivers you might catch channel bass, croakers, catfish, spot, sea trout, and whiting. For bait try chicken livers, shrimp, squid, minnows, or worms. The skill of fishing requires patience and a perhaps even a little good luck!

Gg is for golf

Golfing is a favorite sport in the lowcountry. A round of golf consists of 18 holes of play and usually lasts between 4 - 5 hours. The object of the game is to hit the ball down the long green fairway into a hole on the putting green. Some fairways are as long as five football fields. In golf, the person with the lowest score wins! The Heritage Golf Tournament is a PGA golf tournament held on Hilton Head Island each spring at the Harbour Town Golf Links. This famous tournament attracts players from around the world and has raised over $8 million dollars for various lowcountry charities.

Hh is for history

History of the lowcountry can be traced back to the original inhabitants, the Native Americans. Their remnants are still present as evidenced by clay pottery pieces and other artifacts, such as arrowheads and shell rings that can be found in the Lowcountry today. The Gullah people are descendants of different tribes from the Windward Coast of West Africa. These peoples were often left alone on the sea islands to work on the large rice, cotton, and indigo plantations and were forced to develop their own language in order to communicate with each other. The Gullah language is a mixture of pidgin English, West African words such as 'yams' and 'gumbo,' and the lilting syntax and intonation of a creole language. Many Gullah traditions are alive today such as cooking, spiritual practices, sweet-grass basket weaving, and long-strip quilting. During the Civil War, many Union troops were headquartered on Hilton Head Island. In 1862, Mitchelville, the nation's first freedman's municipality was set up on Beach City Road. The same year, Northern Missionaries began the "Port Royal Experiment," creating schools for the formerly enslaved Africans. One of the most well known and historically significant is the Penn School located on St. Helena Island.

I i is for islands

Islands are bodies of land surrounded by water. There are approximately 35 barrier islands along the coast of South Carolina. They are called barrier islands because they serve as a buffer or barrier to protect the mainland from hurricanes, strong winds, and storms. Hilton Head is the second largest barrier island off the Atlantic Coast. Daufuskie Island is located one nautical mile from Hilton Head and is accessible only by boat or plane. More than 200 residents live on Daufuskie Island and approximately 30 students still attend school on the island today.

Jj is for jellyfish

Jellyfish can often be found washed up on the beach or floating in the ocean. The most common jellyfish is the firm, round Cannonball or Cabbage Head jellyfish. This type has a short stalk with arms and is usually harmless. Another common jellyfish is the Moon jellyfish easily identifiable by its clear disc-shaped body with a beautiful brown star pattern in the center; this jelly can produce a mild sting. The Portuguese Man O' War is a cousin to the jellyfish family and perhaps the most threatening. Its long tentacles may grow up to 6 feet in length and can inflict painful stings. Winds and currents can bring them near the lowcountry shores. During peak season, the shore patrol will post advisories to warn beachgoers of the presence of jellyfish.

Kk is for kudzu

Kudzu is a dense green plant that thrives in the lowcountry. It is very hard to get rid of kudzu once it starts growing. It is aggressive and hardy, often suffocating other natural plants and flora. Another interesting plant is Spanish Moss which is seen hanging from southern oak trees. Spanish Moss is an air plant, which means that it derives all of its nutrients from the rain and sun. Spanish Moss is home to chiggers, little bugs that can bite and burrow into human flesh causing severe discomfort and itching. The old saying, "don't let the bedbugs bite" comes from the days when people used to stuff their mattresses with Spanish Moss only to later suffer uncomfortable chigger bites.

Ll is for lighthouse

Lighthouses provide beacons of light to alert boats and guide them into safe harbors. The first lighthouse in SC was built in 1767 on Morris Island in Charleston. Many lighthouses have interesting histories and have been restored for their lowcountry heritage and charm. The Harbour Town Lighthouse on Hilton Head is a famous landmark. It was not actually built as a "lighthouse," but rather as a tourist attraction under the direction of Charles Fraser, one of the original developers of Sea Pines Plantation. It was known as "Fraser's Folly" as many people doubted the attraction of a lighthouse. Today it is one of the most widely recognized lighthouses in the United States. The Haig Point lighthouse on Daufuskie Island is another picturesque lighthouse that has been authentically restored to its original condition and today serves as a cozy cottage for guests.

Mm is for marsh

Marsh land is one of the most distinctive features of the lowcountry. This salt marsh surrounds many of the barrier islands and is how the lowcountry got its name. The lowcountry refers to the low-lying land of swamps, marshes, and rivers near the coast. At high tide the marsh is flooded near the tips of the grass while at low tide, the marsh is emptied of water revealing the natural mudflats and their oyster beds. The marsh is a very healthy environment for many plants and animals such as fiddler crabs and oysters. Oysters were at one time the primary industry for Daufuskie Island until pollution contaminated the oyster beds in the 1950's. Oysters served in restaurants or markets today are either farm-raised or carefully chosen from selected oyster beds up and down the coast.

Nn is for nature

Nature and her resources provide the lush lifestyle of the lowcountry. From the planned communities, to environmental awareness organizations, and the county and state parks, the mission is the same: to protect and preserve the lowcountry environment. The golden rule for the lowcountry is: to leave it the way you found it. Don't play on the sand dunes, don't disturb the native creatures, and always pick up your trash!

Oo is for ocean

Ocean waters tease the shore of the lowcountry and beckon us to admire and enjoy her beauty. The saltwater of the lowcountry is a greenish-brown color, which means that it is healthy and teeming with rich plant and animal life. Ocean waters rise and fall twice each day, giving us two high flood tides and two low ebb tides in a 24-hour period. At low tide, the beach seems to increase in size allowing us to explore many of the natural tidal pools. The tides are caused by the pull of gravity from the moon and by the land formations of our coastline. As the earth rotates around the sun, the moon pulls the water away from the coast. The further north or south you are from the equator, the greater the tidal pull. Ocean waters vary in depth from a few feet to a few miles. Ocean currents help determine the winds and temperatures affecting the climates throughout the world.

 P p is for palmetto tree

Palmetto or small palm trees abound in the lowcountry. They are the South Carolina state tree and give South Carolina the nickname of the "Palmetto State." They do not bear coconuts like their palm relatives, but they do bear a seed-like fruit for small animals like birds and raccoons to eat. Other local trees include magnolias, pines, and the live oak which is known as the Georgia state tree. In addition to trees, flowers abound in the lowcountry: camelias, gardenias, jasmine, and hydrangeas. Each spring, residents and visitors to the lowcountry look forward to the annual blossoms of the Azalea bush: vibrant hues of pink, purple, red, and white. Their colorful display brilliantly proclaims the arrival of the new season!

Qq is for quahog clam

Quahog clams are one of the most common and easily identifiable seashells found on our shores. This thick-shelled clam is tan or white with fine circular rings revealing the age of the clam. The South Carolina state shell is the lettered olive shell notable for its unusual cylinder shape and smooth shiny finish. The largest local shell is the Whelk shell, a relative of the conch shell and like the conch, it can also be used as a signal horn. It is important to remember that these beautiful shells are not just decorations; they are actually homes for the animals living inside! Sand Dollars may also be found on the beach at low tide but they aren't shells at all; they are sea urchins! Shell collecting is a fascinating hobby that requires care and consideration as it is against the law to remove any living creatures from the beach.

Rr is for reptile

Reptile literally means "to creep" and the lowcountry is home to many creatures that creep. The largest local reptile is the alligator and one of the smallest is the anole, a chameleon-like lizard who changes its color to blend in with the environment. Reptiles are animals that have scales, breathe air, lay eggs with shells out of water and hibernate. They are dependent on the temperature of our climate to regulate their own body metabolism which is why turtles and alligators are often seen sunning themselves on the banks of lagoons. Now don't let a frog fool you! A frog is not a reptile but an amphibian characterized by its smooth skin and the jelly-like eggs they lay in the water rather than on land. A lowcountry favorite is the bright green tree frog; an entertaining creature who can cling to glass doors and windows with its suction-like feet. Despite its tiny size, the green tree frog produces a large croak!

 **is for shrimp boat**

Shrimp boats are a magnificent sight to behold. There is something almost mystical about a shrimp boat trawling our shores with its nets cast and a flock of seagulls trailing behind. Three common species of shrimp are found in our waters: pink, white and brown. Shrimping season occurs from June through December. There are specific regulations to protect and preserve the recreational and commercial shrimping industries. If you don't have a shrimp boat, you can still catch them by casting a net from a local dock. If your shirmping is successful, you can make some Frogmore Stew: a traditional dish of shrimp, sausage, and corn!

Tt is for turtle

Turtles can be seen sunning themselves on the banks of lagoons or swimming in the water. These are Diamondback turtles and if you get close enough you can count the rings around the diamonds on its shell to determine its age. These turtles sleep underwater and eat small fish. You might not see a snapping turtle but they also live in the freshwater ponds and can crush their prey with their powerful beaks. Another local turtle is the Loggerhead sea turtle, which is enormous in size growing up to 4 feet and weighing over 400 pounds. They swim effortlessly in the oceans and may be seen on the beach at night during mating season. They lumber ashore to dig a deep hole and deposit their eggs. Loggerhead turtles are an endangered species and federal law protects them.

Uu is for ultra-violet rays

Ultra-violet rays radiate from the sun; they warm the earth and brighten our days. It is important to remember protection from the sun such as sunscreen, hats, and sunglasses, as overexposure to ultra-violet rays may cause sunburn or skin cancer. The sun rises in the east between 5:30 - 6:30 am and sets in the west as early as 5:00 pm in the winter and as late as 9:00 pm in the summer. Glorious lowcountry sunsets in hues of red and orange are a sight to behold!

Vv is for vacation

Vacations in the lowcountry are a treat for millions of tourists each year. These vacations can include romping on sandy beaches, exploring historical sites, playing golf or tennis, and exploring the natural environment. Tourism is one of the lowcountry's largest industries drawing millions of visitors to Beaufort, Hilton Head Island, Charleston, and Myrtle Beach, South Carolina each year. The coastal towns of Georgia such as Jekyll Island, St. Simon's Island, and Savannah, along with other nearby communities and resorts, also attract thousands of visitors each year. Many former tourists who vacationed in the lowcountry have now become permanent residents!

W w is for weather

Weather in the lowcountry is generally mild and pleasant with average daily temperatures of 55° in the winter and 90 - 95° in the summer. Rain is typically heaviest during the month of August. Hurricanes are large tropical storms that originate out at sea. Hurricanes can result in coastal flooding, whipping winds, and soaking rain. Hurricane season is June through November each year, peaking in the months of September and October. Hurricanes are given alphabetical names by the weather service. Hurricane warnings should be heeded and evacuation of coastal areas may be necessary.

Xx marks the spot

X marks the spot where I live in the lowcountry. The lowcountry is the low-lying land of the coastal regions of Georgia and South Carolina. This region is found on the southeastern portion of the United States map. The lowcounty is just 500 miles from our nation's capital, Washington DC. Many people travel by car to reach the lowcountry; driving from the state of Ohio can take over 10 hours! Traveling here from as far away as Wisconsin or Maine can take almost 20 hours! No matter how you get to the lowcountry or how long it takes you, most will agree, it is definitely worth the trip!

Yy is for yacht

Yachts are large ships that are frequently seen offshore or in many local harbors and marinas. Some yachts are 30 - 100 feet long and can cost millions of dollars. There are more than 10 full-service marinas in Hilton Head and Beaufort, South Carolina alone; each with a varying number of boat slips depending on each harbor's size. Another popular watercraft is the kayak, which is quite the opposite of the luxurious yacht! It is small and sits low to the water like a canoe with room enough for just one or two persons to paddle their way around exploring the lowcountry shoreline. When spending time on any boat it is always necessary to wear a life jacket and know the rules of water safety.

Zz is for zooplankton

Zooplankton is a microscopic animal that is part of the foundation of the rich marine life of the coastal waters. Some zooplankton are bioluminescent, which means they actually "glow in the dark" like fireflies. This twinkling of light in the ocean waters is best observed late at night during the warm summer months and is truly a magical experience!

Twinkling waters and glowing suns are just some of the wonders of the lowcountry. Explore, discover, and enjoy them all!

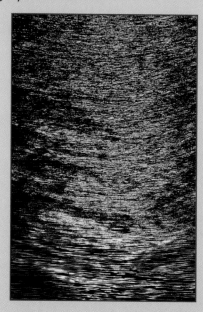

About the Author

Betsy Strickland

Betsy Strickland lives on Hilton Head Island, SC with her husband Arnold Pagatpatan and their two children. She is a contributing writer and the editor of *LowCountry Family Magazine*. She received a BA degree in Journalism from the University of South Carolina, as well as a Master's degree in Speech Pathology.

"The inspiration for **Lowountry A to Z** came from my sons questions about the area. Since then, we have as a family, explored our surroundings: identifying shells, collecting rocks, walking in the mud, observing creatures, and in general, just opening our eyes to the wonders around us!

With Eric Horan's captivating photography and expertise, **LowCountry A to Z** has come to life as a true celebration of the lowcountry…and for this, I am truly grateful."

About the Photographer

Eric Horan

Eric Horan is a commercial photographer based in Beaufort, South Carolina. He graduated from the Colorado Mountain College in Glenwood Springs with a degree in Commercial Art and Photography. He works in the editorial, corporate and commercial advertising markets.

He has received awards from: Carnegie Museum's Natural World Photographic Exhibition, Studio Magazine's International Annual Design Competition, Timberpeg's Annual Architectural Award for Photographic Excellence, South Carolina Wildlife Magazine's Annual Wildlife Photography Exhibition, and the Piccolo Spoleto Festival Art Exhibition.

National publications where his work has appeared include *Business Week, Cruising World, Fortune, McCall's, New York Times Sunday Travel, Outside, Sail, Smithsonian, Tennis,* and *Time.*

Book publications include *South Carolina, A Compass American Guidebook* (a Fodor's Publication), *EXPOSURE,* (100 of Outside Magazine's finest photographs over 15 years), and *Writers Digest.* Besides **Lowcountry A to Z**, Eric has just completed work on **Carolina Nature: A photographer's view of the natural history in the Carolinas**, a tabletop photographic collection of his work from the last fifteen years working in the region.

In addition, Eric has produced the *Lowcountry Wall Calendar* since 2000. Each year it showcases 24 of his natural history photographs from the coastal southeast and features an annual tide chart covering the region from St. Augustine, Florida to Cape Hatteras, North Carolina.

Eric's photographic products available online include: art prints, books, mousepads, notecards, posters and his annual Lowcountry wall calendar. www.southernlight.biz

Credits

- Permission to use the Harbour Town Lighthouse and Golf Links courtesy of The Sea Pines Resort: pgs. 17, 27, 46 and 52.
- *Tree Frog* photo courtesy of Doug Gardner ©2003: p. 42.
- Author's photograph courtesy of Matthew Gardiner / Raffisson Studio Photography.